National Geographic KiDS

My First
Atlas of the World

NATIONAL GEOGRAPHIC

WASHINGTON, D.C.

My First Atlas of the World

North America 14

South America 20

EARTH TO GLOBE

When astronauts travel into space, they see that planet Earth is really an enormous round ball. A globe is a small, round model of Earth. On a globe you see the planet as the astronauts do—one side at a time.

EARTH

4

GLOBE

To see what's on the other side of a **globe,** all you have to do is turn it. ▶

EARTH AS A MAP

A map is a flat drawing of Earth. A world map lets you see the whole Earth at one time. This map shows water in blue and land in green. The biggest pieces of land are called continents. The largest areas of water are called oceans.

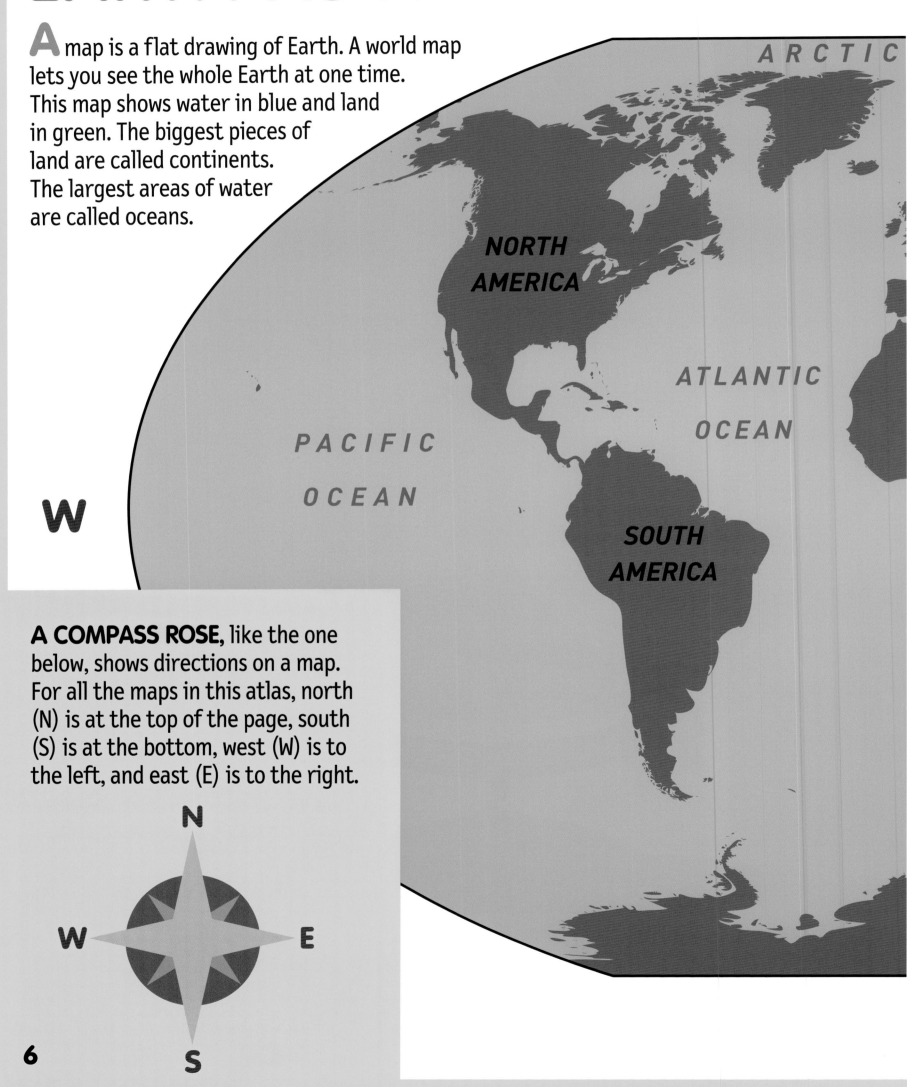

ARCTIC

NORTH AMERICA

ATLANTIC OCEAN

PACIFIC OCEAN

W

SOUTH AMERICA

A COMPASS ROSE, like the one below, shows directions on a map. For all the maps in this atlas, north (N) is at the top of the page, south (S) is at the bottom, west (W) is to the left, and east (E) is to the right.

N

W   E

S

6

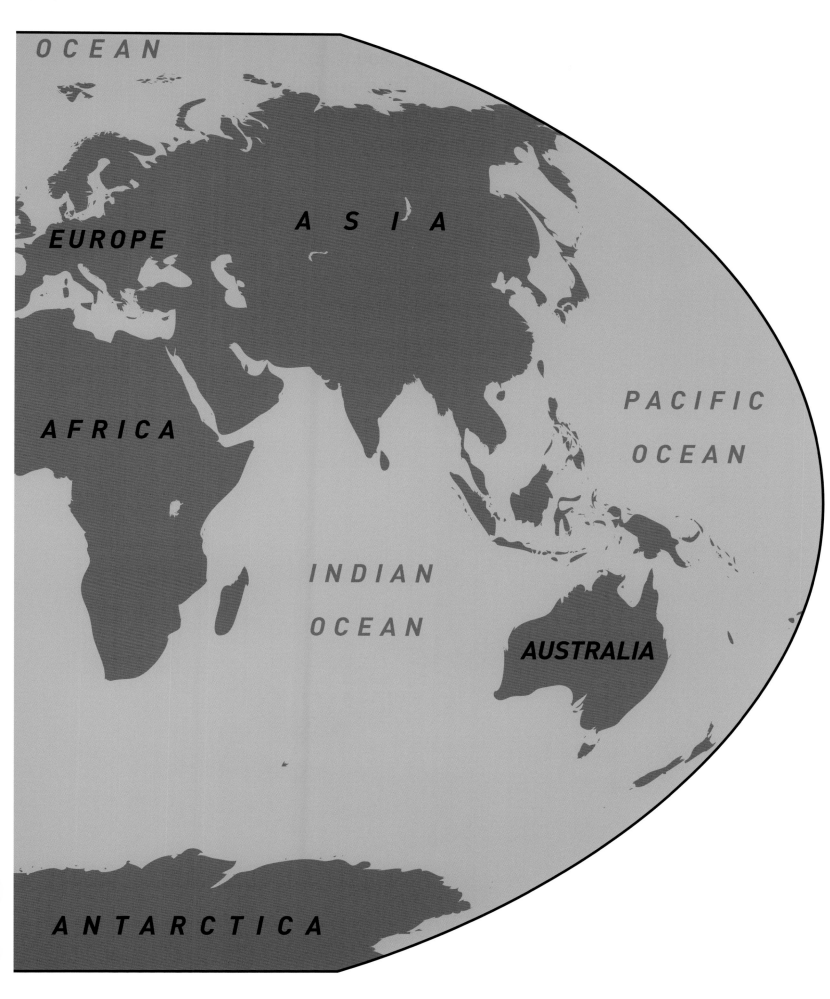

OCEAN

EUROPE

ASIA

AFRICA

PACIFIC

OCEAN

INDIAN

OCEAN

AUSTRALIA

ANTARCTICA

LOOKING AT THE LAND

Land is not flat like a sheet of paper. It has high and low places. Trees grow in forests. Grasslands fill low open spaces. Mountains and volcanoes are high. Deserts are dry. Oceans and lakes are full of water, and rivers sometimes have waterfalls as they flow to lower ground. Can you find these features in this drawing?

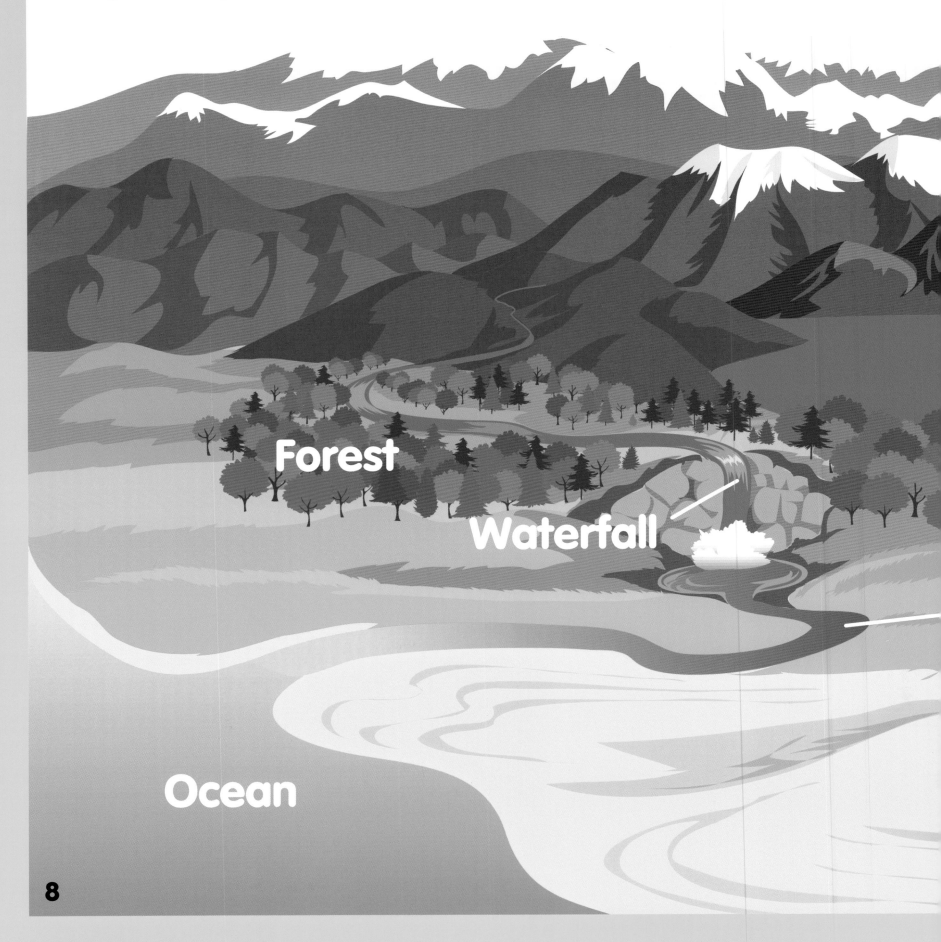

Forest

Waterfall

Ocean

Mountain

Volcano

Lake

Grassland

River

Desert

LAND AND WATER

A map can't show everything, so it uses tiny drawings, called symbols, to show what Earth's surface looks like. A map key, like the one below, tells you what the symbols on a map mean. Map labels are used to name some of Earth's most important features.

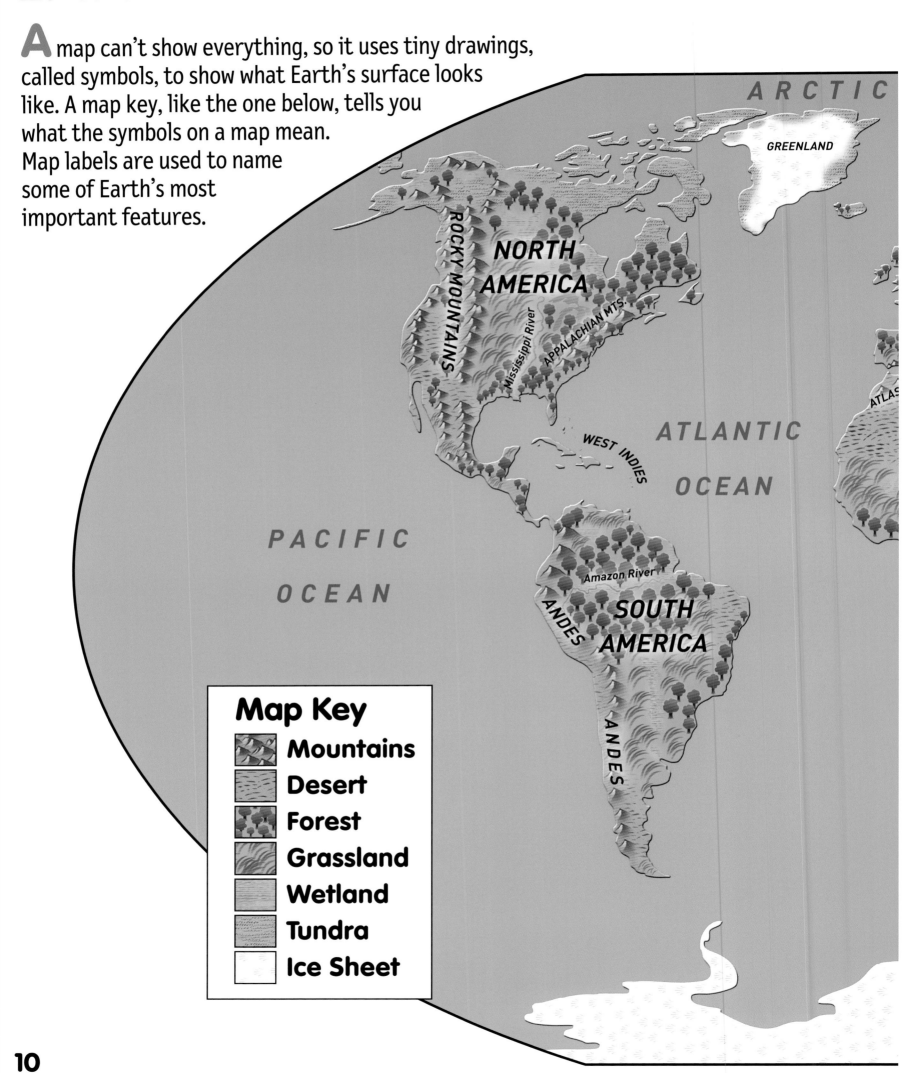

ARCTIC

GREENLAND

ROCKY MOUNTAINS

NORTH AMERICA

Mississippi River

APPALACHIAN MTS.

ATLAS

ATLANTIC OCEAN

WEST INDIES

PACIFIC OCEAN

Amazon River

ANDES

SOUTH AMERICA

ANDES

Map Key
- Mountains
- Desert
- Forest
- Grassland
- Wetland
- Tundra
- Ice Sheet

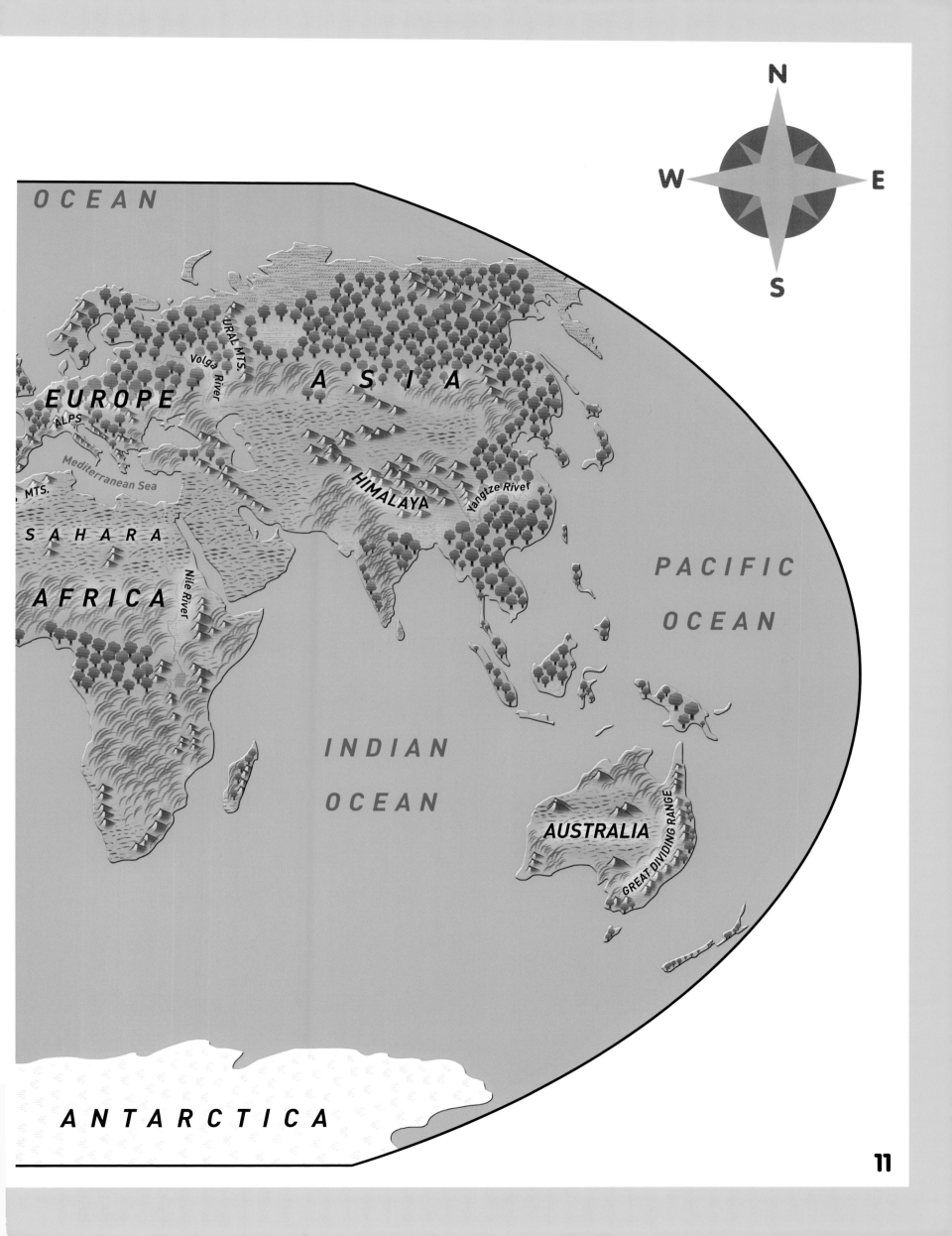

WHERE PEOPLE LIVE

People have divided Earth's surface into many different countries. What country do you live in? Can you find it on the map? This map shows countries in different colors so it's easy to see where one country ends and another begins. This map uses labels to name many—but not all—of the countries in the world. To see the countries on each continent, keep reading.

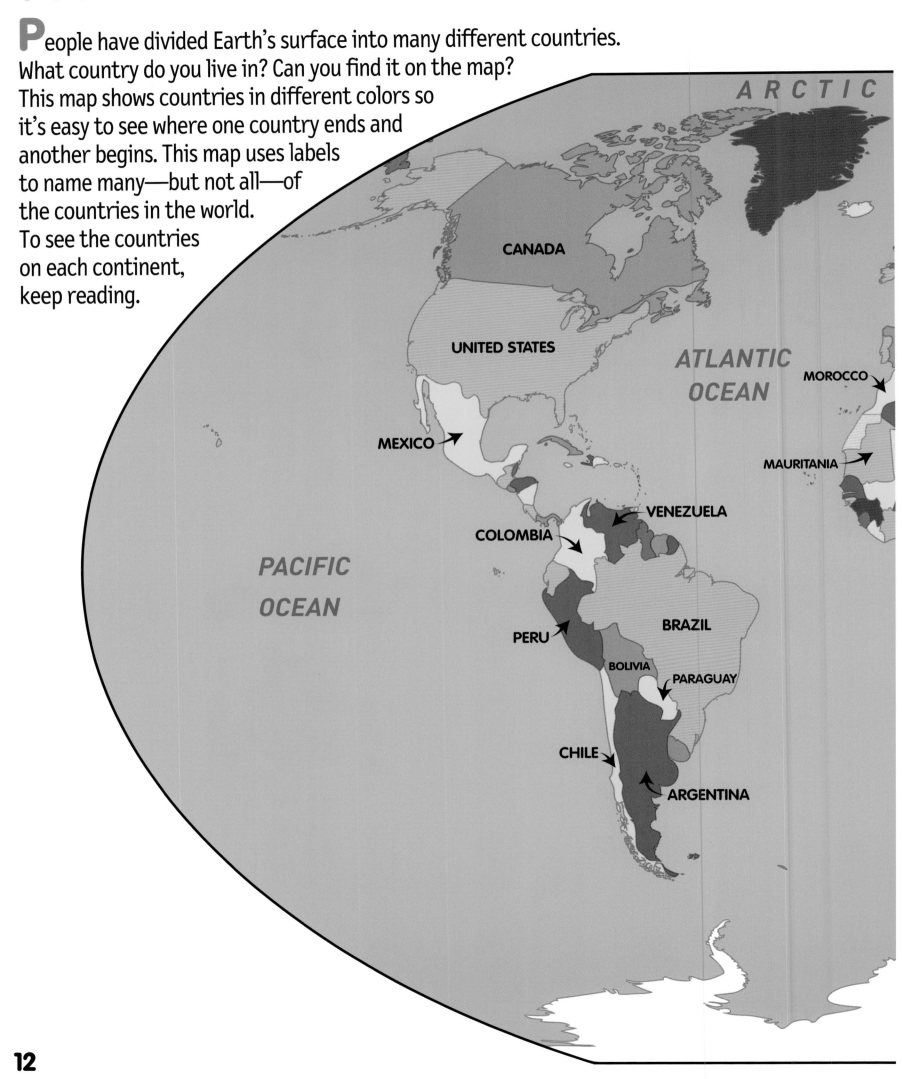

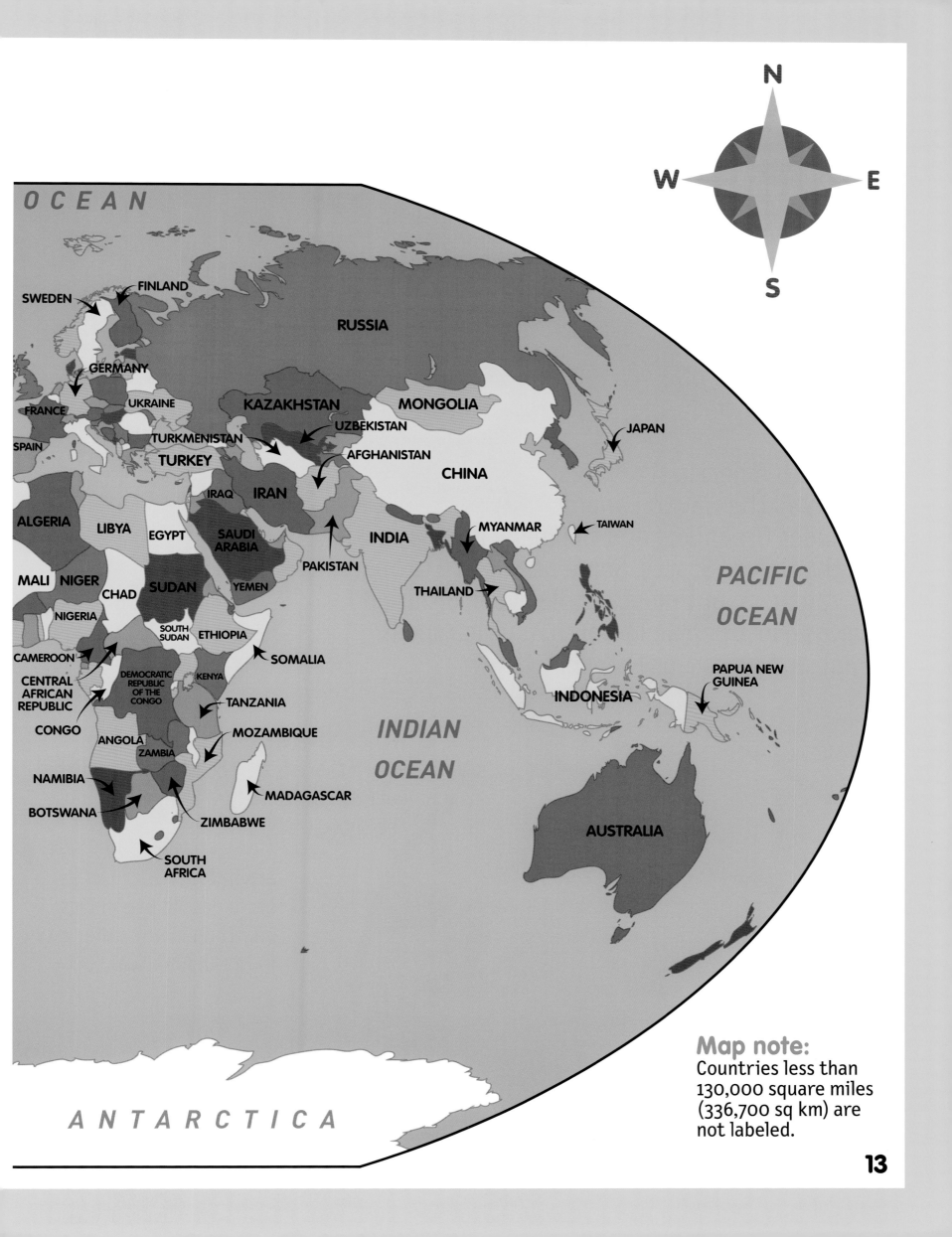

OCEAN

N
W E
S

SWEDEN
FINLAND
GERMANY
FRANCE
UKRAINE
SPAIN
TURKMENISTAN
TURKEY
ALGERIA
LIBYA
EGYPT
IRAQ
IRAN
SAUDI ARABIA
MALI
NIGER
CHAD
SUDAN
YEMEN
NIGERIA
SOUTH SUDAN
ETHIOPIA
CAMEROON
CENTRAL AFRICAN REPUBLIC
DEMOCRATIC REPUBLIC OF THE CONGO
KENYA
SOMALIA
CONGO
TANZANIA
ANGOLA
MOZAMBIQUE
ZAMBIA
NAMIBIA
BOTSWANA
ZIMBABWE
MADAGASCAR
SOUTH AFRICA

RUSSIA
KAZAKHSTAN
MONGOLIA
UZBEKISTAN
AFGHANISTAN
CHINA
JAPAN
PAKISTAN
INDIA
MYANMAR
TAIWAN
THAILAND

PACIFIC OCEAN

PAPUA NEW GUINEA
INDONESIA

INDIAN OCEAN

AUSTRALIA

ANTARCTICA

Map note:
Countries less than
130,000 square miles
(336,700 sq km) are
not labeled.

NORTH AMERICA

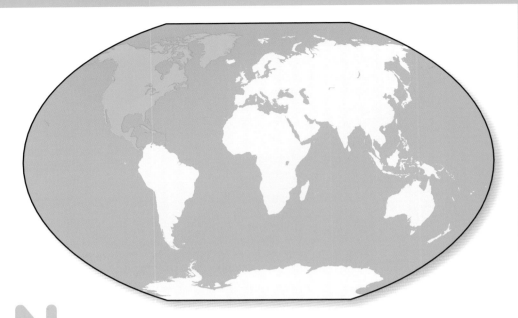

WAITING FOR SCHOOL IN CUBA

North America stretches from Canada in the north all the way to Panama in the south. It also includes Greenland and the many islands south of the United States. Some people are farmers or ranchers, but most people live in cities and towns. Most people in North America speak English, Spanish, or French.

◀ **Polar bears** live in the far north where there is ice and snow most of the year. White fur helps them hide against the snow.

These crowded buildings are in **Mexico City.** More people live in this city than in any other city in North America. ▶

ON THE MAP!

Denali is North America's highest mountain. It is in Alaska. **Can you find Alaska?**

Tiny hummingbirds live in the tropical forests of Costa Rica's mountains. **Where is Costa Rica?**

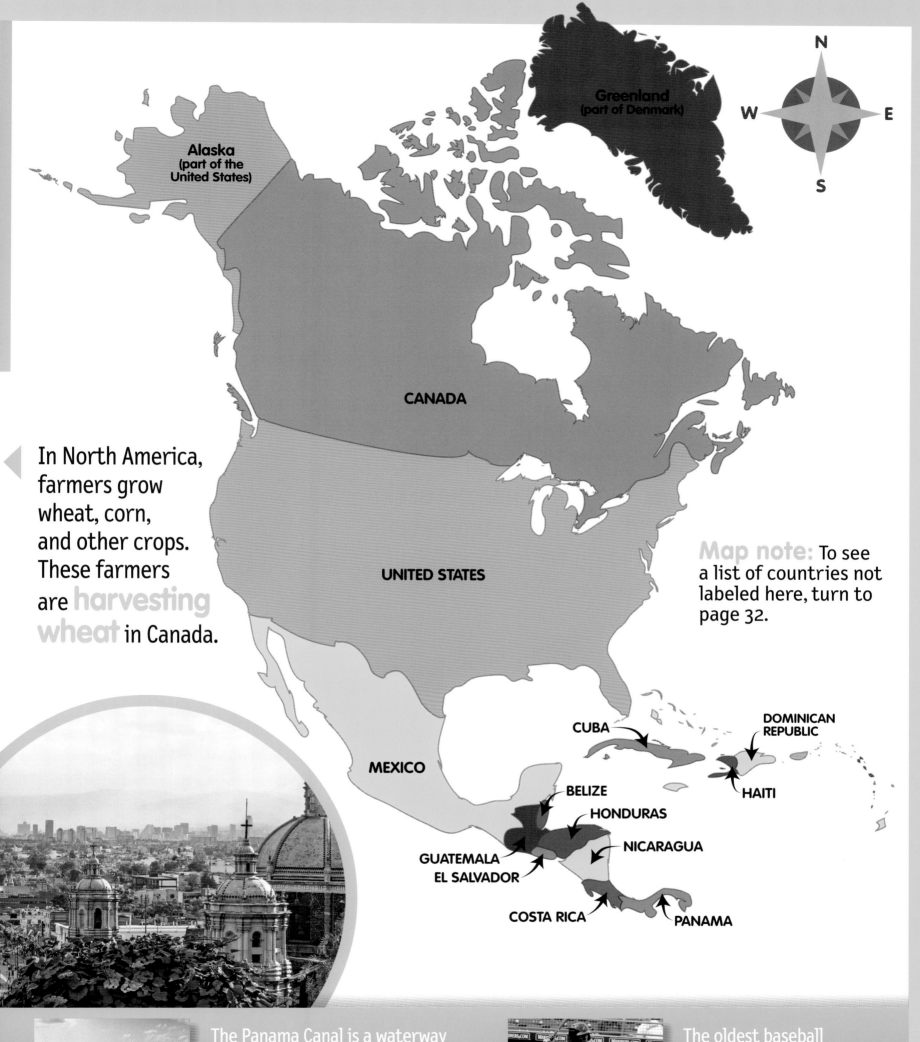

Greenland
(part of Denmark)

Alaska
(part of the
United States)

CANADA

In North America, farmers grow wheat, corn, and other crops. These farmers are **harvesting wheat** in Canada.

UNITED STATES

Map note: To see a list of countries not labeled here, turn to page 32.

MEXICO

CUBA

DOMINICAN REPUBLIC

BELIZE

HAITI

HONDURAS

NICARAGUA

GUATEMALA
EL SALVADOR

COSTA RICA

PANAMA

The Panama Canal is a waterway that runs through Panama. Ships use it as a shortcut between the Atlantic and the Pacific Oceans. **Can you find Panama?**

The oldest baseball team in the United States is the Atlanta Braves. **Where is the United States?**

15

UNITED STATES

LITTLE LEAGUE BASEBALL PLAYERS IN MINNESOTA

The United States is part of North America. People from all over the world live here. The country is made up of 50 states that extend from Maine to Hawai'i and from Alaska to Florida.

Tornadoes are powerful, funnel-shaped winds. They sometimes happen during thunderstorms. The United States has more tornadoes than any other country in the world.

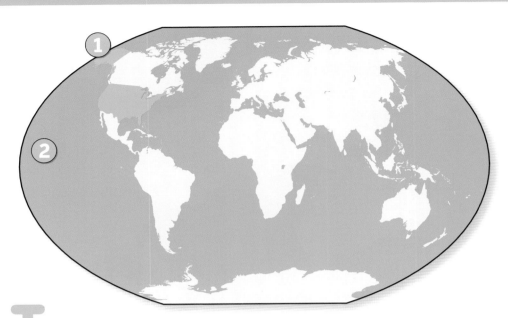

A **rocket** lifts off from the space center in Florida. The United States uses rockets to deliver supplies to astronauts on the International Space Station.

ON THE MAP!

There are many volcanoes in Hawai'i and Alaska. Washington, Oregon, and California have some, too. **Can you find all five states?**

The Everglades is a huge swampy place in Florida. Alligators, birds, and lots of other animals live there. **Where is Florida?**

N
W E
S

Washington
Montana
North Dakota
Minnesota
New Hampshire
Vermont
Maine
Oregon
Idaho
Michigan
Massachusetts
Connecticut
New York
Wisconsin
Wyoming
South Dakota
Rhode Island
Nevada
Nebraska
Iowa
Pennsylvania
Ohio
New Jersey
Utah
Indiana
Delaware
Maryland
California
Colorado
Illinois
West Virginia
Virginia
Washington, D.C.
Kansas
Missouri
Kentucky
North Carolina
Arizona
New Mexico
Oklahoma
Arkansas
Tennessee
South Carolina
Mississippi
Alabama
Georgia
Texas
Louisiana
Florida

Alaska
1

Hawaiʻi
2

Map note: To see the real location of the states of Alaska and Hawaiʻi, look at the small world map (top left).

The president of the United States lives in the White House. It is in Washington, D.C., the capital city. ▶

The Statue of Liberty stands at the entrance to New York Harbor. This symbol of freedom welcomes people to the United States. **Can you find New York?**

Old Faithful is a spout of hot water and steam. It shoots out of the ground in Yellowstone National Park in Wyoming. **Where is Wyoming?**

17

CANADA

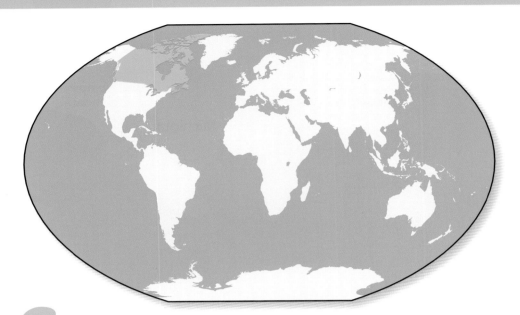

PLAYING ICE HOCKEY IN CANADA

Canada is the largest country in North America. It has lots of wide-open spaces. Native people called Inuit live in cold northern Canada. Polar bears live there, too. Most people live in cities that are much farther south. The main languages are English and French.

Winterlude is a festival held in Ottawa, Canada's capital city. It celebrates winter with snow sculptures, the world's longest ice-skating rink, and a playground made of snow!

Moose are the largest members of the deer family. They live throughout much of Canada near lakes and streams and in forests.

ON THE MAP!

Native people in British Columbia carve colorful totem poles to tell stories about their history. **Can you find British Columbia?**

Cowboys ride horses and bulls at the Calgary Stampede. This special event takes place each summer in Alberta. **Where is Alberta?**

Yukon

Northwest Territories

Nunavut

Newfoundland and Labrador

British Columbia

Alberta

Saskatchewan

Manitoba

Quebec

Prince Edward Island

Ontario

New Brunswick

Nova Scotia

N
W   E
S

◀ The **Rocky Mountains** in western Canada are a popular vacation spot. People come to canoe, hike, ski, and climb the rugged mountains.

The Canada lynx, a wild member of the cat family, lives in the snowy forests of northern Canada. **Can you find northern Canada?**

The Canadian National Tower is the tallest tower in North America. It is one of Canada's most famous places. It is in Toronto, Ontario. **Where is Ontario?**

SOUTH AMERICA

SCHOOLGIRLS IN ECUADOR

South America is made up of 12 countries and one French territory. Brazil is the largest country. People in Brazil speak Portuguese. In almost every other country in South America, people speak Spanish. The north has warm, tropical rain forests. In the south, mountains are covered with snow.

Cowboys called gauchos ▶ herd cattle in grassy areas of Argentina and Uruguay. Beef is a popular food in South America.

◀ **Jaguars** are South America's largest wild cat. **Macaws** are big, colorful birds. They both live in the rain forests of South America.

ON THE MAP!

Angel Falls is the highest waterfall in the world. To see it, you'd have to hike through the rain forest in Venezuela. **Can you find Venezuela?**

Machu Picchu is an ancient city located high in the Andes Mountains. Native people built it long ago in Peru. **Where is Peru?**

VENEZUELA

GUYANA

SURINAME

French Guiana
(part of France)

COLOMBIA

ECUADOR

Galápagos
Islands
(part of Ecuador)

PERU

BRAZIL

BOLIVIA

Farmers in Ecuador
ship **bananas**
to markets all over
the world.

PARAGUAY

Every year people celebrate
a festival called **Carnival**
in Brazil. They dress up in
colorful costumes and parade
through the streets.

CHILE

URUGUAY

ARGENTINA

Falkland
Islands
(part of the
United
Kingdom)

N
W E
S

Llamas are good at climbing
mountains. People in Bolivia
and other mountainous
countries in South America
use them to carry things.
Can you find Bolivia?

The Amazon is a huge river
that flows from the Andes
Mountains across Brazil to the
Atlantic Ocean. It carries more
water than any other river.
Where is Brazil?

EUROPE

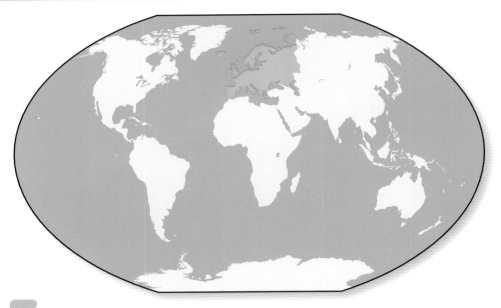

BAKING MUFFINS IN GERMANY

Europe has many countries with different languages and people. It has many long fingers of land called peninsulas that stick out into the sea. There are lots of islands and long rivers. This means no place is very far from the water.

PORTUGAL

SPAIN

Venice is a city in Italy with many canals. People there often travel along the city's canals in boats called **gondolas.**

This woman is picking **grapes.** Many kinds of fruit grow in southern Europe, where the weather is often warm and sunny.

ON THE MAP!

St. Basil's is the most famous church in Russia. Its colorful rooftops are called onion domes because of their shape. **Can you find Russia?**

Iceland has more than 100 volcanoes and many hot springs. It also has huge rivers of ice called glaciers. **Where is Iceland?**

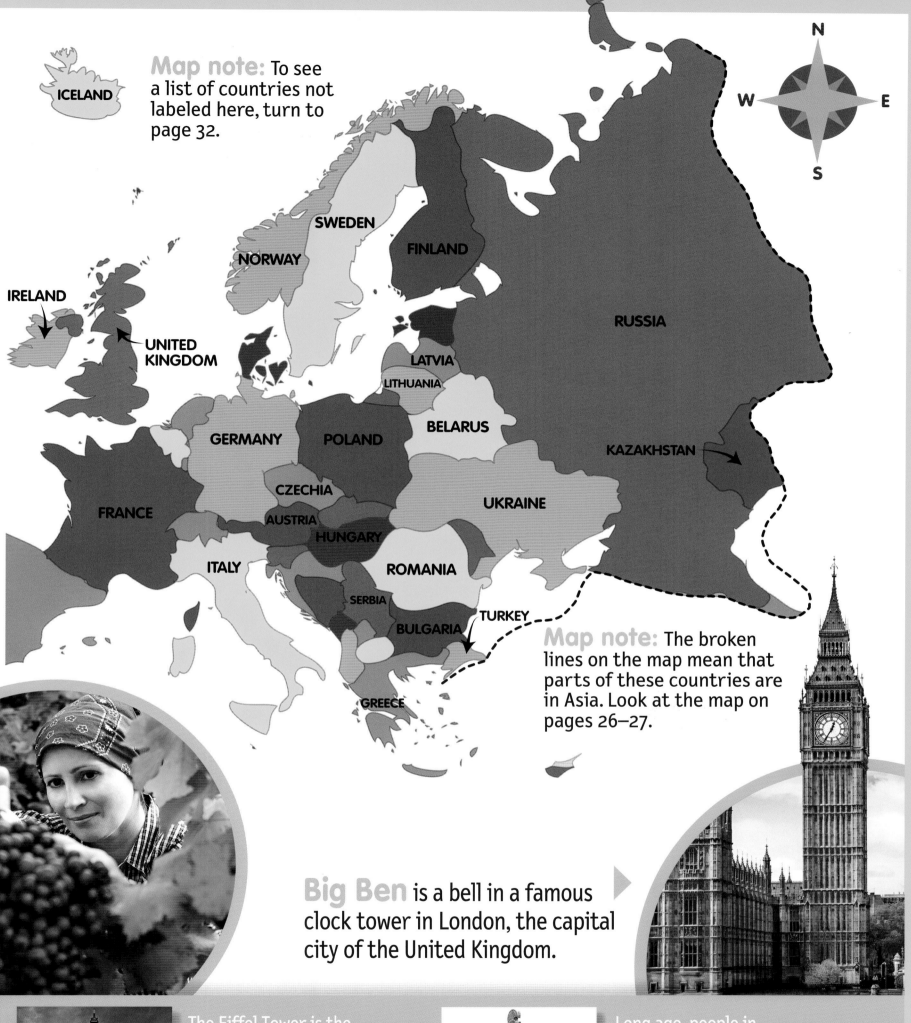

Map note: To see a list of countries not labeled here, turn to page 32.

ICELAND

N
W   E
S

IRELAND

UNITED KINGDOM

SWEDEN

NORWAY

FINLAND

RUSSIA

LATVIA

LITHUANIA

BELARUS

KAZAKHSTAN

GERMANY

POLAND

FRANCE

CZECHIA

AUSTRIA

HUNGARY

UKRAINE

ITALY

ROMANIA

SERBIA

BULGARIA

TURKEY

GREECE

Map note: The broken lines on the map mean that parts of these countries are in Asia. Look at the map on pages 26–27.

Big Ben is a bell in a famous clock tower in London, the capital city of the United Kingdom.

The Eiffel Tower is the tallest structure in Paris, France. It is a favorite stop for tourists visiting Paris.
Can you find France?

Long ago, people in Greece believed gods and goddesses ruled Earth. Athena was the goddess of wisdom and war.
Where is Greece?

AFRICA

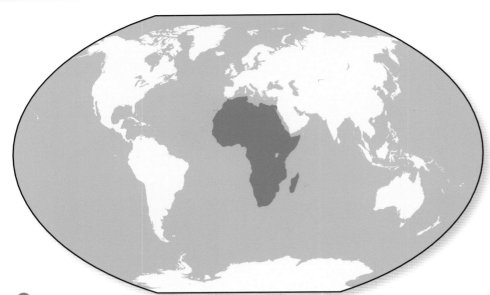

SAMBURU GIRLS IN KENYA WEAR BEADED JEWELRY.

Africa has 54 countries—more than any other continent. The people there speak more than a thousand different languages. Africa has hot deserts, tropical rain forests, and open grasslands. Many people are farmers or herders. Other people live in towns or large cities.

Only male **lions** have a thick mane of hair around their heads. Lions live on Africa's grasslands in family groups called prides.

ON THE MAP!

Mount Kilimanjaro is Africa's highest mountain. This snow-capped mountain is in Tanzania. **Can you find Tanzania?**

People living in Egypt long ago built the pyramids. When their rulers died, they were buried in pyramids. **Where is Egypt?**

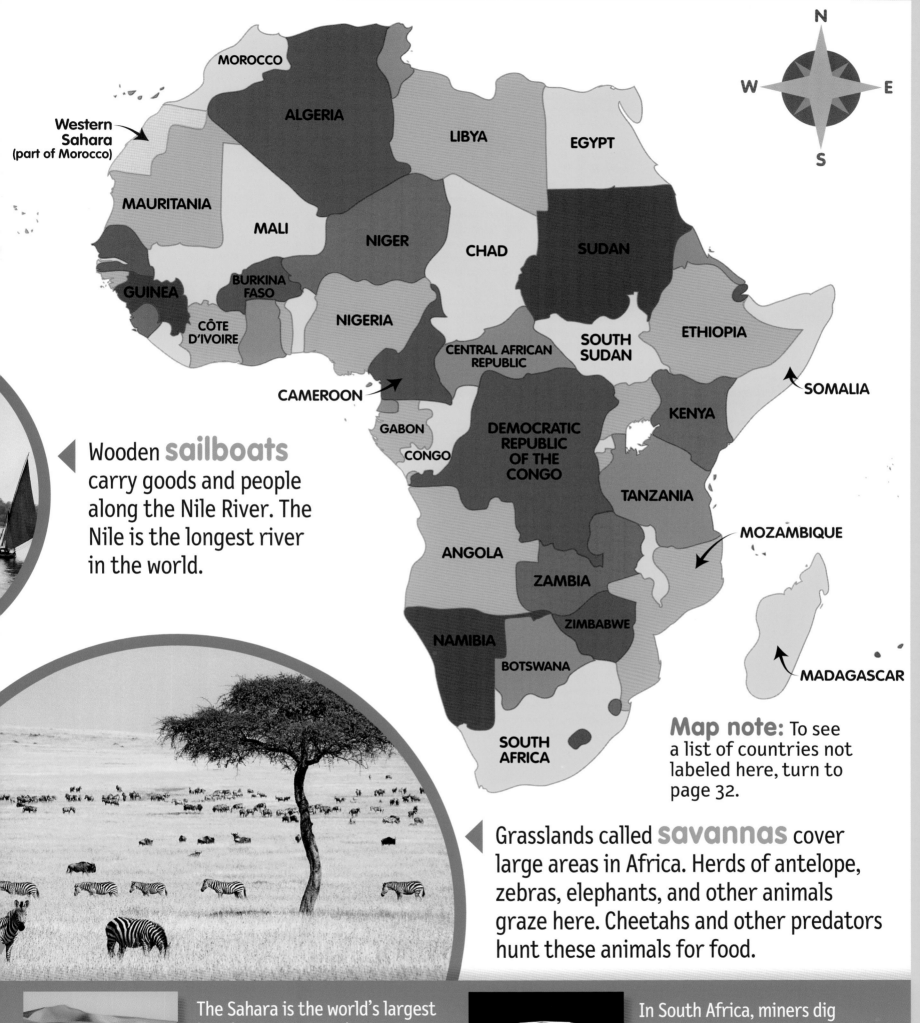

Western Sahara (part of Morocco)

MOROCCO

ALGERIA

LIBYA

EGYPT

MAURITANIA

MALI

NIGER

CHAD

SUDAN

GUINEA

BURKINA FASO

CÔTE D'IVOIRE

NIGERIA

CENTRAL AFRICAN REPUBLIC

SOUTH SUDAN

ETHIOPIA

SOMALIA

CAMEROON

GABON

CONGO

DEMOCRATIC REPUBLIC OF THE CONGO

KENYA

TANZANIA

MOZAMBIQUE

ANGOLA

ZAMBIA

ZIMBABWE

NAMIBIA

BOTSWANA

MADAGASCAR

SOUTH AFRICA

◀ Wooden **sailboats** carry goods and people along the Nile River. The Nile is the longest river in the world.

Map note: To see a list of countries not labeled here, turn to page 32.

◀ Grasslands called **savannas** cover large areas in Africa. Herds of antelope, zebras, elephants, and other animals graze here. Cheetahs and other predators hunt these animals for food.

The Sahara is the world's largest hot desert. It stretches across much of northern Africa from Mauritania to Egypt. Some people use camels to cross it. **Can you find Mauritania?**

In South Africa, miners dig for diamonds, gold, and other valuable minerals. Mining is a dangerous job. **Where is South Africa?**

ASIA

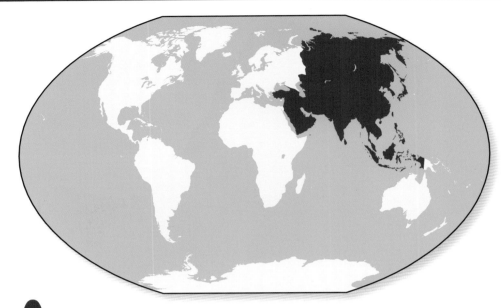

SKIPPING THROUGH A PARK IN BALI, INDONESIA

Asia has the most people, the most land, and the highest mountains on Earth. There are large deserts, hot rain forests, and even frozen tundra. Some countries, like Japan, are islands. Other countries, like Mongolia, are far from the ocean.

◀ **Bamboo** is the giant panda's favorite food. These animals live in the wild only in China in places where bamboo forests grow.

ON THE MAP!

Many people in India believe the Ganges River has healing power. Sick people bathe in its waters in order to get well. **Where is India?**

The city of Jerusalem in Israel is an important religious center for Jews, Christians, and Muslims. **Where is Israel?**

Map note: The broken lines on the map mean that parts of these countries are in Europe. Look at the map on pages 22–23.

N
W   E
S

RUSSIA

TURKEY

ISRAEL

KAZAKHSTAN

JAPAN

IRAQ

UZBEKISTAN

TURKMENISTAN

MONGOLIA

IRAN

AFGHANISTAN

SAUDI ARABIA

PAKISTAN

CHINA

Map note: To see a list of countries not labeled here, turn to page 32.

NEPAL

TAIWAN

YEMEN   OMAN

INDIA

PHILIPPINES

Mount Everest is the highest mountain in the world. It is almost six miles (10 km) high! It is located on the border between Nepal and China.

MYANMAR

VIETNAM

THAILAND

MALAYSIA

INDONESIA

Rice is a main food eaten in Asia. Some farmers grow it on steplike fields called terraces. These fields are cut into steep hillsides.

The Great Wall of China was built hundreds of years ago to keep out enemies. It is more than 5,000 miles (8,050 km) long. **Can you find China?**

Japan's fastest trains are called bullet trains. The trains carry millions of people to and from work each day. **Can you find Japan?**

AUSTRALIA

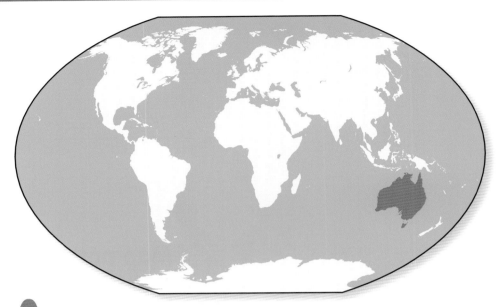

SNORKELING IN QUEENSLAND, AUSTRALIA

Australia is the smallest continent. It also has just one country—Australia! Water is all around Australia. Its Great Barrier Reef is full of all kinds of sea life. In the middle of Australia is a desert with very little water. Australia has animals that are found nowhere else on Earth.

The roof of the **Sydney Opera House** looks like sails on a boat. Sydney is Australia's largest city.

Many roads in Australia are straight and flat. Drivers here have to be on the look-out for **kangaroos** that may come bounding across the road!

ON THE MAP!

The Snowy Mountains are the highest mountain range in Australia. They receive heavy snow in the winter. **Where are the Snowy Mountains?**

The Tasmanian devil raises its young in a pouch on its belly. It is called "devil" because it makes screamlike noises. **Can you find Tasmania?**

Map note: Because Australia is both a continent and a country, additional information is added to its map.

N
W E
S

Great Barrier Reef

AUSTRALIA

Uluru
(Ayers Rock) ▲

Sydney ●

Snowy Mountains ▲

Tasmania

◄ The cuddly-looking **koala** lives in the wild only in Australia. Koalas eat leaves of the eucalyptus tree. They sleep 18 hours a day.

The Great Barrier Reef is the longest coral reef in the world. It lies in shallow ocean waters off Australia's east coast. **Where is the Great Barrier Reef?**

Ayers Rock rises from the desert in the middle of Australia. It is far from any large city. The native people call it Uluru. **Can you find Uluru?**

ANTARCTICA

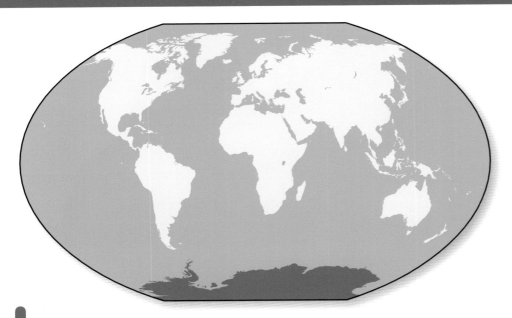

EMPEROR PENGUIN AND CHICK IN ANTARCTICA

If you visited Antarctica, you would see penguins and seals, snow-covered mountains and valleys, and ice. The continent is so cold that people come only for visits, not to live. There aren't any cities, but you would find scientists at work. Antarctica is the only continent that has no countries.

Scientists come to Antarctica from other continents. These scientists traveled from Italy to study how emperor penguins live in such a cold climate. ▶

◀ This **leopard seal** is ready to dive for penguins under the ice. Many kinds of animals live in the ocean around Antarctica.

ON THE MAP!

Antarctica has mountains and even some volcanoes. Mount Erebus is the world's southernmost volcano. **Where is Mount Erebus?**

The South Pole is the southernmost point on Earth. It is marked by flags and a pole. **Can you find the South Pole?**

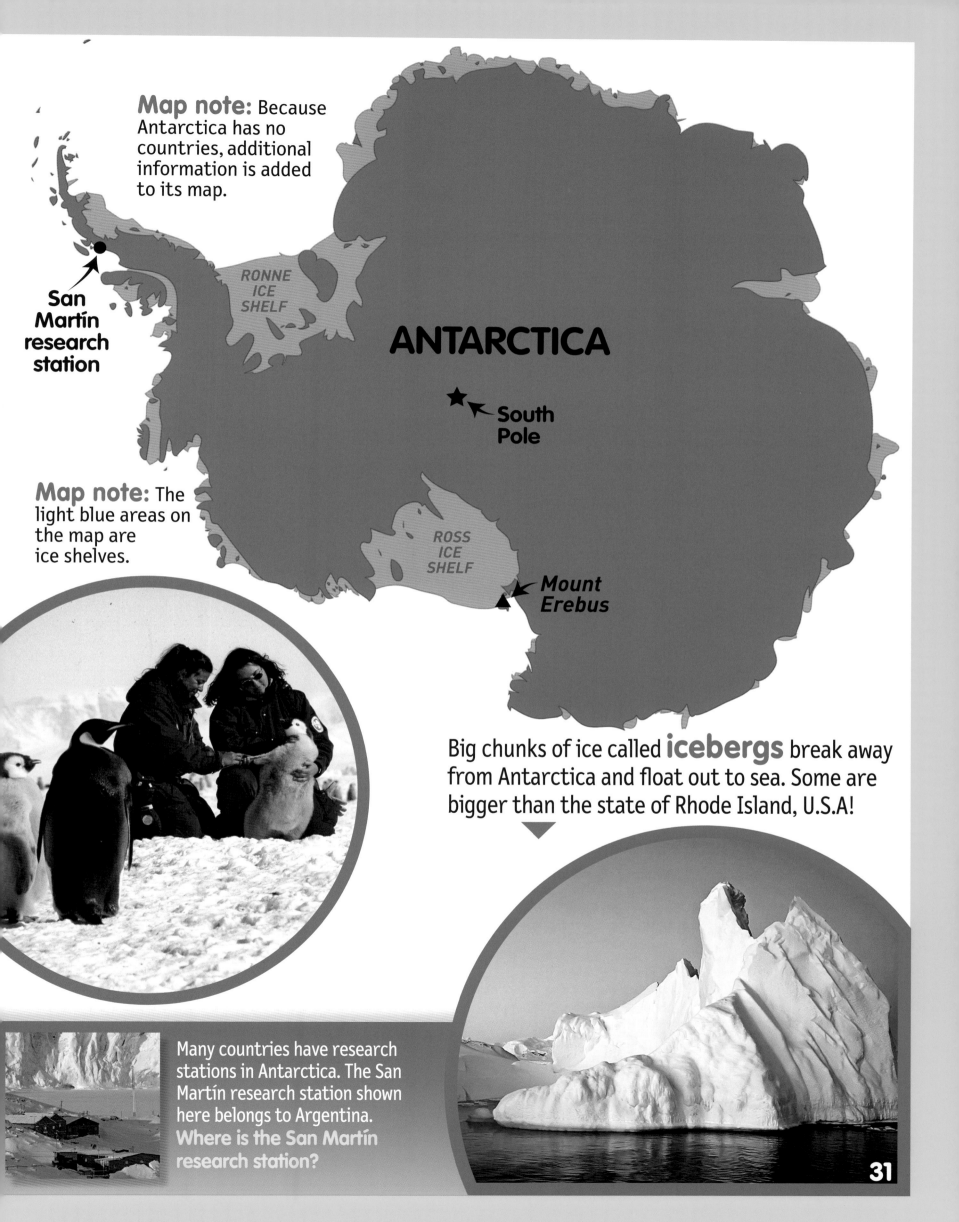

Map note: Because Antarctica has no countries, additional information is added to its map.

San Martín research station

RONNE ICE SHELF

ANTARCTICA

South Pole

Map note: The light blue areas on the map are ice shelves.

ROSS ICE SHELF

Mount Erebus

Big chunks of ice called **icebergs** break away from Antarctica and float out to sea. Some are bigger than the state of Rhode Island, U.S.A!

Many countries have research stations in Antarctica. The San Martín research station shown here belongs to Argentina. **Where is the San Martín research station?**

GLOSSARY

canal A canal is a narrow waterway that people have built across the land. The Panama Canal was built across the country of Panama.

capital city A capital city is the place where a country's government is located. Washington, D.C., is the capital city of the United States.

coast A coast is land that borders an ocean.

desert A desert is a place that gets very little rain or snow. It can be sandy or rocky, hot or cold. The Sahara is the world's largest hot desert.

ice sheet An ice sheet is a permanent sheet of thick ice that covers land. Greenland and Antarctica both have ice sheets.

ice shelf An ice shelf is a thick sheet of ice that sticks out beyond the land into the sea. The largest ice shelves are in Antarctica.

lake A lake is a body of water that is surrounded by land.

mountain A mountain is the highest kind of land. Mount Everest is the highest mountain.

peninsula A peninsula is a piece of land that sticks out into the water. Italy and Florida, U.S.A., are examples of peninsulas.

predator A predator is an animal that hunts other animals.

rain forest A rain forest is a woodland that grows in a place that is very wet and usually quite warm. The Amazon rain forest is the largest in the world.

river A river is a large stream of water that flows across the land. The Nile is the world's longest river.

tundra Tundra is a cold region with low plants that grow only during a short warm season.

volcano A volcano is an opening in Earth's surface through which melted rock from deep inside Earth forces its way out onto the surface. Some mountains are volcanoes.

wetland A wetland is an area of land, such as a swamp or a marsh, that is mostly covered with water. The Everglades, in Florida, U.S.A., is a wetland.

PRONUNCIATION GUIDE

Note: The accented syllable is in capital letters.

Ayers	airz	**gauchos**	GOW-choz
Carnival	kar-nih-VAL	**gondolas**	GAHN-duh-luz
Denali	duh-NAH-lee	**Himalaya**	hih-MAHL-yuh
Erebus	ER-uh-bus	**Kilimanjaro**	kih-lih-mun-JAR-o
eucalyptus	you-kuh-LIP-tus	**Tasmanian**	taz-MAY-nee-un
Ganges	GAN-jeez	**Uluru**	oo-LOO-roo

UNLABELED COUNTRIES ON CONTINENT MAPS

Page 15, Countries less than 8,000 square miles (20,720 sq km)
Antigua and Barbuda, Bahamas, Barbados, Dominica, Grenada, Jamaica, Saint Kitts and Nevis, Saint Lucia, Saint Vincent and the Grenadines, Trinidad and Tobago

Pages 22–23, Countries less than 24,000 square miles (62,160 sq km)
Albania, Andorra, Belgium, Bosnia and Herzegovina, Croatia, Cyprus, Denmark, Estonia, Kosovo, Liechtenstein, Luxembourg, Macedonia, Malta, Moldova, Monaco, Montenegro, Netherlands, San Marino, Slovakia, Slovenia, Switzerland, Vatican City

Page 25, Countries less than 94,000 square miles (243,460 sq km)
Benin, Burundi, Cabo Verde, Comoros, Djibouti, Equatorial Guinea, Eritrea, Gambia, Ghana, Guinea-Bissau, Lesotho, Liberia, Malawi, Mauritius, Rwanda, Sao Tome and Principe, Senegal, Seychelles, Sierra Leone, Swaziland, Togo, Tunisia, Uganda

Page 27, Countries less than 100,000 square miles (259,000 sq km)
Armenia, Azerbaijan, Bahrain, Bangladesh, Bhutan, Brunei, Cambodia, Georgia, Jordan, Kuwait, Kyrgyzstan, Laos, Lebanon, Maldives, North Korea, Qatar, Singapore, South Korea, Sri Lanka, Syria, Tajikistan, Timor-Leste, United Arab Emirates

Note: Israel and Nepal are each less than 100,000 square miles (259,000 sq km), but are labeled on the page 27 Asia map because they are discussed in the text.

PHOTO CREDITS

GI = Getty Images; NG = National Geographic Image Collection; SS = Shutterstock
Cover (parrot), Vladimir Melnik/SS; (frog), Photolukacs/SS; (pyramids), sculpies/SS; (totem), JJS-Pepite/GI; (penguins), TravelMediaProductions/SS; (statue), photoDISC; (butterfly), Paul Reeves Photography/SS; back cover (UP LE), aabeele/SS; (UP RT), Debra James/SS; (CTR LE), Pola Damonte/SS; (CTR RT), Gecko1968/SS; (LO LE, LO RT), photoDISC; 4, leonello/GI; 5 (LO RT), Comstock; 14 (UP), akturer/SS; 14 (CTR LE), Gecko1968/SS; 14 (CTR RT), J. Baylor Roberts/NG; 14 (LO LE), photoDISC; 14 (LO RT), drferry/GI; 15 (CTR LE), Jess Kraft/SS; 15 (LO LE), Peek Creative Collective/SS; 15 (LO RT), Keeton Gale/SS; 16 (UP), Steve Skjold/Alamy Stock Photo; 16 (CTR LE), NASA/Tony Gray and Sandra Joseph; 16 (CTR RT), Minerva Studio/SS; 16 (LO LE), AZ68/GI; 16 (LO RT), Don Mammoser/SS; 17 (CTR RT), Vacclav/SS; 17 (LO LE), AG-PHOTOS/SS; 18 (UP), Lorcel/SS; 18 (UP), Hero Images/GI; 18 (CTR LE), Michal_K/SS; 18 (CTR RT), Carl & Ann Purcell/GI; 18 (LO LE), JJS-Pepite/GI; 18 (LO RT), Steve Estvanik/SS; 19 (CTR), BrianAJackson/GI; 19 (LO LE), Lynn_Bystrom/GI; 19 (LO RT), Russell Marini/SS; 20 (UP), Hugh Sitton/GI; 20 (CTR LE), Mikadun/SS; 20 (CTR CTR), Vladimir Melnik/SS; 20 (CTR RT), Alexander Mazurkevich/SS; 20 (LO LE), Alice Nerr/SS; 20 (LO RT), Dan Breckwoldt/SS; 21 (CTR LE), O. Louis Mazzatenta/NG; 21 (CTR RT), CP DC Press/SS; 21 (LO LE), robertcicchetti/GI; 21 (LO RT), Janne Hamalainen/SS; 22 (UP), Niedring/Drentwett/GI; 22 (CTR), Iakov Kalinin/SS; 22 (LO LE), alex83/SS; 22 (LO RT), Emory Kristof/NG; 23 (CTR LE), SurkovDimitri/GI; 23 (CTR RT), S.Borisov/SS; 23 (LO LE), WDG Photo/SS; 23 (LO RT), Dimitrios/SS; 24 (UP), Bartosz Hadyniak/GI; 24 (CTR LE), Michael Potter11/SS; 24 (CTR RT), OSORIOartist/SS; 24 (LO LE), Graeme Shannon/SS; 24 (LO RT), WitR/SS; 25 (CTR), erichon/SS; 25 (LO LE), eAlisa/SS; 25 (LO RT), 123dartist/SS; 26 (UP), Cedric Lim/GI; 26 (CTR LE), Hung Chung Chih/SS; 26 (CTR RT), Daniel Prudek/SS; 26 (LO LE), Yotir/GI; 26 (LO RT), ESB Professional/SS; 27 (CTR), photoDISC; 27 (LO LE), Hung Chung Chih/SS; 27 (LO RT), Nikada/iStockPhoto; 28 (UP), ChameleonsEye/SS; 28 (CTR LE), JohnCarnemolla/GI; 28 (CTR RT), Nadezda Zavitaeva/SS; 28 (LO LE), Greg Brave/SS; 28 (LO RT), Flash-ka/SS; 29 (CTR), Anne B. Keiser/NG; 29 (LO LE), Debra James/SS; 29 (LO RT), Stanislav Fosenbauer/SS; 30 (UP), TravelMediaProductions/SS; 30 (CTR), Achim Baque/SS; 30 (LO LE), Andrew H. Brown/NG; 30 (LO RT), Frank Whitney/GI; 31 (CTR), Vittoriano Rastelli/Corbis via GI; 31 (LO LE), estanux/SS; 31 (LO RT), Volodymyr Goinyk/SS

Published by National Geographic Partners, LLC.

First edition copyright for Our World:
A Child's First Picture Atlas © 2000 National Geographic Society
Updated copyright © 2006 National Geographic Society
Second edition as My First Atlas of the World copyright © 2018
National Geographic Partners, LLC

Since 1888, the National Geographic Society has funded more than 14,000 research, conservation, education, and storytelling projects around the world. National Geographic Partners distributes a portion of the funds it receives from your purchase to National Geographic Society to support programs including the conservation of animals and their habitats. To learn more, visit natgeo.com/info.

For more information, visit nationalgeographic.com, call 1-877-873-6846, or write to the following address:

National Geographic Partners, LLC
1145 17th Street N.W.
Washington, DC 20036-4688 U.S.A.

For librarians and teachers: nationalgeographic.com/
books/librarians-and-educators
More for kids from National Geographic: natgeokids.com

For rights or permissions inquiries, please contact
National Geographic Books Subsidiary Rights:
bookrights@natgeo.com

Martha B. Sharma, Writer and Researcher
Catherine D. Hughes, Early Childhood Consultant
Kathryn Robbins, Designer

The publisher would like to thank everyone who worked to make this book come together: Angela Modany, associate editor; Hilary Andrews, associate photo editor; Mike McNey, map production; Scott A. Zillmer, map research and edit; Sean Philpotts, production director; Anne LeongSon and Gus Tello, design production assistants; Sally Abbey, managing editor; and Molly Reid, production editor.

Hardcover ISBN: 978-1-4263-3174-9
Reinforced library binding ISBN: 978-1-4263- 3175-6

Printed in South Korea
22/ISK/6